SYSTEM INTEGRATORS GUIDE *to* WIN HIGH-TICKET ORDERS

Grow 10X and Become Markets First Choice

SYSTEM INTEGRATORS GUIDE *to* WIN HIGH-TICKET ORDERS

Grow 10X and Become Markets First Choice

ATUL MODI ANUJ MODI

Worldwide Published by

Pendown Press

PENDOWN PRESS LLP

An ISO 9001 & ISO 14001 Certified Co.

Regd. Office 3767A, Kanhaiya Nagar,
Tri Nagar, Delhi-110035
Ph.: 8130886000, 9650072927, 8595249536
E-mail: info@pendownpress.com
Branch Office 1A/2A, 20, Hari Sadan, Ansari Road,
Daryaganj, New Delhi-110002
Ph.: 011-45794768
Website: PendownPress.com

First Edition: 2023
Price: ₹499/-
ISBN: 978-93-5554-686-9

Special Thanks

We're grateful to Akshar Yadav, our marketing guru. His inclusive approach, belief in authenticity, and mentorship transformed us. His emphasis on marketing for positive change inspired us. We thank him wholeheartedly for igniting transformative growth and creating inclusive marketing experiences.

CONTENTS

Hi, we are Atul Modi, Director, and Anuj Modi, CEO of MIPL (AXL). Both of us are successful entrepreneurs running a brand aimed at enhancing individuals' mobility and technology experience. We have taken on the challenge of overseeing the marketing, sales, and operations of the company, and demonstrated expertise in these areas through our 20 years of experience in marketing and sales.

Our technical background, honed through exposure to the IT industry, makes us experts in operations and marketing automation, and valuable assets to the team. We are active members of ISODA (Infotech Software Dealers Association). Atul has played various roles, including North Regional Secretary and Chairperson of the Tech Summit. In the Delhi-based IT association PCAIT (Progressive Channel Association of Information Technology), Anuj held the position of Joint Secretary for six years, showing our commitment to the industry. We continue to take part in the association's meetings, learning daily practices from our dealer community.

Our dedication to the industry has been recognized through awards from NCN, Var India, and Mobility magazine. These accolades honor us for developing a top brand under the Make in India initiative. Additionally, our accomplishments as a writer of **"System Integrators Guide to Win High-Ticket Orders"** contribute to making our organization a well-rounded and valuable member of the business community.

In addition to our professional achievements, we are dedicated to improving the business environment and regularly meet with government bodies to provide suggestions for ease of doing business and GST compliance. The respect we have gained as valuable members of the business community, combined with our passion for entrepreneurship and commitment to excellence, makes us inspiring leaders.

OUR PASSION

We are passionate entrepreneurs and writers with MBA in Marketing and Finance. Our fascination with solving day-to-day business challenges and the impact they have on our modern world led us to write this book. We have spent years studying and exploring the legacies of various business organizations, and we are excited to share our insights with you.

In this book, you will learn how organizations, by not following the current sequence and making mistakes, hinder their ability to generate the profits they are entitled to and how it impacts their world. Through engaging stories and vivid illustrations, we will take you on a journey of discovery, revealing the common practices entrepreneurs must adapt to organize their daily routines.

We are excited to share our passion for this subject with you, and we hope you will join us on this journey of learning and discovery.

THIS BOOK IS FOR

This book can be read by anyone for whom growth in business is important, regardless of their reasons, especially those in the field of Information Technology, specifically System Integration.

You are possibly one of them:

1. A business owner of an SME or a System Integrator.

2. A professional or consultant looking to implement technology and business strategies.

OUR JOURNEY

We are Atul Modi and Anuj Modi, and along with our family members, we run a family-owned business in IT distribution and system integration. Our brand is known for its quality and reliability. Growing up, we saw our father's tireless work to provide comfortable living for our family and expand his business. He always had a deep passion for technology and the products he sold, and from a young age, we knew we wanted to be a part of that world.

Our father has been involved in the business of importing and distributing computer peripherals for the past 35 years. He, along with our uncles, were among the early importers of computer peripherals in India, and they eventually began distributing these products as well. They promoted several international brands of laptops, desktops, printers, and other computer peripherals.

However, our father soon realized that these brands were not really supportive of their efforts. Initially, they would provide support and push for product promotion, but as soon as the product gained popularity, they would supply the same product to our competitors, making it difficult for us to grow in the market.

It was at this point that our father made the decision to start something of his own and create a homegrown brand. In 2016, he founded AXL & MIPL and we began importing accessories. It took us two years and multiple visits to different factories to find the right quality and good factory. We focused on importing power banks, which quickly became popular. Recently, we have also launched Make in India- based notebooks, and we have plans to expand into servers and Desktop in the near future.

I remember the day we received our first shipment of accessories. Our father was so excited and proud, and I could see the passion and determination in his eyes. He was creating something of his own, something that he believed in and something that would make a difference in the lives of others.

With the success of the accessories, we continued to introduce new products, and our potential was huge. We saw that we had a great opportunity to grow, and we seized it. Today, we have sold more than 3.5 million units and have more than 3.5 million customers. We have a strong team of 50 people who are dedicated to providing our customers with great quality products that they can rely on.

AXL & MIPL has become synonymous with quality and reliability, and we take immense pride in the excellence of our products and the reputation we have earned. Our customers know that when they buy an AXL & MIPL product, they are getting a great product that they can trust. This is what sets us apart from our competitors and has made us one of the leading brands in the market.

But for me, AXL & MIPL is much more than just a brand. It's a story of hard work, dedication, and commitment to providing our customers with the best products possible. It's a story of our father's passion for technology and his unwavering commitment to both his family and customers. And it's a story that I am proud to be a part of, as we continue to grow and make a difference in the lives of others.

WHY THIS BOOK

We are writing this book to enhance the lives of business owners, as it is crucial to share valuable knowledge and experience in the field. The insights and lessons we have got can benefit others in the technology industry and potentially improve their processes, practices, and overall success. By documenting and sharing these experiences, we are contributing to the growth and development of the technology industry. Furthermore, this book can serve as a reference and resource for professionals in the field, fostering innovation and progress.

Initially, we had intended to share these insights with only our top 15 distributors. However, we have realized that limiting the growth of our country's economy is not in line with our responsibilities as a responsible citizen and entrepreneur. This book represents our small effort to contribute to our country, which has given us so much. We are proud to be an Indian Citizen.

SOME RECENT STATS

90 percent

Furthermore, the minister highlighted that the number of recognized startups in India has increased from 452 in 2016 to 84,012 in 2022. It is worth noting that almost 90 percent of startups worldwide face failure, with 10 percent of them failing within the first year. Many of these failed startups are distribution-led businesses that encounter challenges due to a lack of proper execution.

According to data from the Bureau of Labor Statistics, as reported by Fundera, approximately 20 percent of small businesses fail within the first year. By the end of the second year, the failure rate increases to 30 percent. Within five years, about half of the businesses will have failed. And by the end of the decade, only 30 percent of businesses will remain, resulting in a 70 percent failure rate.

A TRIBUTE TO
OUR INSPIRATION

We are incredibly grateful to Akshar Yadav, our marketing guru whose guidance and inspiration have transformed our lives. His inclusive approach to marketing and unwavering belief in the power of authenticity has reshaped our understanding of creating impactful campaigns and building a strong foundation in our organization. Akshar's mentorship has accelerated our business growth, and his emphasis on marketing practices instead of operations has inspired us to use marketing as a force for positive change. His compassion, empathy, and ability to connect on an emotional and spiritual level have empowered us personally and professionally. We wholeheartedly thank Akshar as a marketing guru who not only ignites transformative growth but also creates inclusive and meaningful marketing experiences.

ACKNOWLEDGEMENTS

Thank you for taking the time to read this book. Special recognition is given to Saurabh Agarwal, Kishan, Rajeev, Jindal and many more for their years of experience in System Integration of products for multiple large organizations and for being entrepreneurs. I also extend gratitude to the current and former team members, including Saumitra, Chandan, Sunil, Simran, Nitish, Kiran, and Rajiv.

I would like to thank each reader for their interest in the book and acknowledge their contribution to the IT industry. I express gratitude to all past colleagues and customers, including those from our time at Samsung, HP, Dell, and others, for providing valuable learning experiences through their challenges and successes. These experiences have allowed me to learn something new, and a part of it is presented in this book.

TESTIMONIALS

"As the CEO of It Simple, my experience with Atul and Anuj's Team has been nothing short of exceptional. Their expertise in sales and marketing strategies has been instrumental in helping us boost our revenue and expand our customer base. Their proactive approach, personalized solutions, and unwavering commitment to customer satisfaction have made them an invaluable partner in our journey."

~Kamal Gulati, It Simple

"As a Director of Operations at Swastik Systems, I have had the pleasure of collaborating with Modi Brothers on multiple projects. Their Insight on sales, marketing, and customer care is a treasure trove of valuable insights and practical tips. Their approach to understanding customer needs and delivering tailored solutions sets them apart from the competition."

~Atul Jain, Swastik Systems

"Atul and Anuj's collaboration transformed XSYS Solutions. Their invaluable book, rooted in industry knowledge, improved client approach, sales, and customer satisfaction. Implementing their insights boosted sales and customer loyalty."

~Aditya Bhasin, XSYS Solutions

7 STEPS TO ACCELERATE YOUR BUSINESS: GROWTH HACK

(1) New age Mindset

a) Communication Care

1. **Active Listening:** Pay close attention to your customers and demonstrate genuine interest in their concerns. Engage in active listening by attentively listening to their questions, feedback, and complaints. This conveys that you value their opinion and are dedicated to comprehending their needs.

2. **Empathy:** Place yourself in your customer's position and strive to grasp their perspective. Display empathy by acknowledging their emotions and concerns. This helps build rapport and fosters a positive customer experience.

3. **Clear and Concise Communication:** Use simple and easy-to-understand language when interacting with customers. Avoid using jargon or technical terms that may cause confusion. Provide concise responses, offering relevant information without overwhelming them with unnecessary details.

4. **Prompt Responses:** Strive to promptly address customer inquiries and messages. If an immediate solution is not available, acknowledge their query and provide an estimated timeframe for resolution. Keeping customers informed helps manage their expectations and demonstrates reliability.

5. **Personalization:** Whenever possible, address customers by their names and tailor your responses to their specific needs or concerns. This personal touch helps create a more personalized and engaging customer experience.

6. **Positive Language and Tone:** Choose your words carefully and maintain a positive and professional tone in your communication. Avoid sounding defensive or confrontational, even in situations where the customer may be frustrated or upset. Maintain a calm and courteous demeanor throughout the conversation.

7. **Offer Solutions:** Instead of simply acknowledging an issue, focus on providing practical solutions to resolve their concerns. Offer clear steps or options to address their concerns. If necessary, involve relevant departments or colleagues to ensure a comprehensive resolution.

8. **Follow-Up:** After successfully resolving a customer's issue, make sure to follow up to ensure their satisfaction and ask for feedback. This gesture demonstrates that you value their opinion and are committed to continuously improving your customer service.

Remember, effective customer care communication is an ongoing endeavor that demands empathy, responsiveness, and a customer-centric approach. By implementing these principles, you can build strong relationships with your customers, ultimately increasing their satisfaction and loyalty.

b) Know your Customer

Knowing your customers is crucial for understanding their needs, preferences, and behaviors. Here are some steps you can take to gain a better understanding of your customers:

1. **Conduct market research:** Use various research methods to gather information about your target audience. This can include surveys, interviews, focus groups, and online research. Determine demographics, psychographics, buying behaviors, and preferences that align with your product or service.

2. **Create buyer personas:** Develop detailed profiles of your ideal customers or buyer personas. These profiles should include information such as demographics, interests, goals, pain points, and purchasing behaviors. Buyer personas help humanize your target audience and provide insights for crafting targeted marketing strategies.

3. **Engage in customer feedback and surveys:** Implement feedback mechanisms to encourage customers to share their opinions, suggestions, and experiences. Use surveys, feedback forms, and online reviews to gather valuable insights directly from your customers. Actively listen and

respond to their feedback to demonstrate that you value their input.

4. **Build relationships and engage in customer conversations:** Actively participate in conversations with your customers. Respond promptly and personally to their inquiries, comments, and concerns. Engage in social media discussions, join relevant online communities, and participate in industry events to establish strong relationships with your customers.

5. **Leverage customer analytics tools:** Utilize customer analytics tools that can provide in-depth insights into customer behavior and preferences. These tools can help you segment your customer base, analyze purchase patterns, and identify opportunities for personalized marketing campaigns.

6. **Stay updated and adapt:** Continuously monitor customer preferences and market trends. Be flexible and willing to adapt your strategies based on changing customer needs and expectations. Regularly evaluate and refine your understanding of your customers to ensure your efforts align with their evolving preferences.

Remember, getting to know your customers is an ongoing process. Regularly revisit and refine your understanding of your target audience to ensure that you stay aligned with their needs and expectations.

***

(2) Building connections

How to build a relationship with a key person in an organization:

1. **Identify the Key person:**

   - Research and identify the key person within the organization who holds influence or decision-making power.

   - Gather information about their background, achievements, areas of expertise, and current responsibilities.

   - Gain an understanding of their priorities, challenges, and goals within the organization.

2. **Find common connections:**

   - Explore if you have any shared connections who can introduce you to the key person.

   - Mutual acquaintances or colleagues can help facilitate an introduction and provide valuable insights about the person you want to build a relationship with.

   - Attend relevant events and networking opportunities:

   - Look for professional events, conferences, or industry gatherings where you might have the opportunity to meet the key person.

   - Take the initiative to introduce yourself and engage in conversations related to their work or organization.

- Show genuine interest in their perspectives and expertise.

3. **Be authentic and genuine:**

   - Approach the relationship-building process with authenticity and genuine interest.

   - Ask open-ended questions to learn more about the key person and their experiences.

   - Actively listen and demonstrate empathy and understanding.

4. **Maintain regular contact:**

   - After the initial introduction, make an effort to stay in touch with the key person to nurture the relationship.

   - Stay connected through occasional emails, invitations for coffee or lunch, or social media platforms like LinkedIn.

   - Respect their time and boundaries, being mindful not to become too intrusive.

5. **Showcase your expertise and value:**

   - Continuously demonstrate your expertise, skills, and value within your field.

   - Share your achievements, success stories, or relevant updates that may be of interest to the key person.

   - Establish yourself as a reliable resource and someone who can contribute to their objectives.

6. **Seek mentorship or guidance:**
   - If appropriate, approach the key person and ask if they would be willing to mentor you or provide guidance in your professional development.
   - Express your admiration for their expertise and ask if they would be open to sharing their insights and experiences.
   - Foster a deeper connection through mentorship or guidance.

7. **Build a personal connection:**
   - Discover shared hobbies, interests, or activities that you can engage in together.
   - Participate in industry-related events or social gatherings to connect on a personal level.
   - Strengthen the bond by building a personal connection alongside the professional one.

8. **Build a network within the organization:**
   - Expand your efforts beyond the key person and connect with other individuals within the organization who may have influence or be valuable contacts.
   - Networking within the organization can strengthen your overall position and increase your visibility.

Remember that building relationships takes time, effort, and patience. The key is to approach the process with sincerity, respect, and a genuine desire to create a mutually beneficial connection.

***

(3) Is customer the King really

Customer is the King Really

Yes, the phrase "customer is king" holds significant meaning in the business world. It underscores the fundamental principle that customers are of utmost importance in any business. This concept emphasizes that a company's success hinges on its ability to satisfy and fulfill the needs of its customers. **When customers are happy and satisfied with a product or service, they are more inclined to remain loyal, make repeat purchases, and recommend the business to others.** Consequently, businesses strive to deliver excellent customer service, personalized experiences, and high-quality products to ensure customer satisfaction and foster long-term loyalty.

Here are a few reasons why the customer is considered king:

1. **Revenue generation:** Customers are the source of revenue for businesses. Without customers, there would be no sales, and consequently, no profits. Satisfied customers are more likely to make repeat purchases and become loyal patrons, contributing to long-term revenue growth.

2. **Market competition:** In today's competitive business landscape, customers have numerous choices available to them. Companies must strive to provide exceptional products, services, and experiences to attract and retain customers. Their preferences and demands drive market dynamics and influence business strategies.

3. **Reputation and brand image:** Customers have the power to shape a company's reputation and brand image through their reviews, feedback, and word-of-mouth recommendations. Positive experiences lead to a favorable brand perception, while negative experiences can damage a company's reputation. Therefore, businesses that prioritize customer satisfaction can cultivate a positive brand image and build trust among consumers.

4. **Feedback and improvement:** Customers provide valuable feedback and insights that help businesses understand their needs, preferences, and expectations. By listening to customer feedback, companies can identify areas for improvement, refine their products or services, and enhance the overall customer experience.

5. **Long-term relationships:** Cultivating strong, long-term relationships with customers is essential for sustainable business growth. Loyal customers not only generate repeat business but also serve as brand advocates, attracting new customers through positive referrals. By prioritizing customer satisfaction and building trust, businesses can foster loyalty and enjoy the benefits of customer retention.

In summary, the phrase "Customer is king" reflects the acknowledgment that customers hold significant power and influence over a business's success. By prioritizing customer satisfaction, businesses can drive revenue, build a positive brand image, foster loyalty, and stay ahead in a competitive marketplace.

***

4) Be the Problem solver

a) Have in depth Knowledge of products and services

IT system integrators should have in-depth product knowledge for several reasons:

1. **Effective Solution Design:** To design and implement an IT solution that meets the specific needs of a client, system integrators must possess a deep understanding of the products and technologies involved. This knowledge enables them to evaluate various options, select the most suitable products, and design a solution architecture that maximizes functionality, performance, and compatibility.

2. **Seamless Integration:** IT system integrators are responsible for integrating various hardware and software components into a cohesive system. With in-depth product knowledge, they can ensure seamless integration between different components, avoiding compatibility issues, data inconsistencies, and system failures. By understanding the technical nuances of each product enables integrators to develop effective integration strategies and troubleshoot any issues that may arise.

3. **Optimal Configuration and Customization:** Products and technologies often offer a wide range of configuration options and customization capabilities. By possessing comprehensive product knowledge, system integrators can identify the most appropriate configuration settings and tailor the solution to meet the specific requirements of

the client. This results in optimized system performance and an enhanced user experience.

4. **Vendor Relationship Management:** System integrators frequently collaborate closely with technology vendors and suppliers. Having a deep understanding of the products allows integrators to effectively communicate with vendors, engage in technical discussions, and advocate for client needs. Building strong vendor relationships can result in improved support, timely updates, and access to the latest product enhancements, ultimately benefiting both the integrator and the client.

In summary, possessing in-depth product knowledge empowers IT system integrators to design optimal solutions, seamlessly integrate components, configure and customize systems effectively, troubleshoot problems efficiently, and manage relationships with vendors. This expertise enhances the integrator's ability to deliver successful projects that meet client expectations and drive business value.

b) How to become a problem solver

Becoming a problem solver involves developing certain skills, adopting a proactive mindset, and applying effective strategies. Here are some steps you can take to enhance your problem-solving abilities:

1. **Develop a growth mindset:** Embrace the idea of a growth mindset, which believes that challenges can be overcome through effort, learning, and perseverance. Cultivate a

positive attitude towards problem-solving, viewing obstacles as opportunities for personal growth and development.

2. **Enhance your critical thinking skills:** Enhancing your critical thinking forms the basis for effective problem-solving. Improve your critical thinking abilities by practicing skills such as analysis, evaluation, logical reasoning, and creative thinking. Seek out opportunities to solve puzzles, engage in debates, and evaluate complex situations.

3. **Generate alternative solutions:** Once you have a clear understanding of the problem, brainstorm and generate multiple alternative solutions. Encourage creativity and think beyond conventional boundaries. Avoid premature judgment or self-censorship during the idea generation phase.

4. **Evaluate and select the best solution:** Evaluate each alternative solution based on its feasibility, potential outcomes, and alignment with desired goals. Consider the advantages and disadvantages of each option. Select the solution that is most likely to address the root cause of the problem effectively.

5. **Implement the chosen solution:** Create a comprehensive action plan to implement the chosen solution. Divide the plan into smaller, manageable steps. Assign responsibilities, set deadlines, and ensure the availability of necessary resources. Take decisive action and monitor progress as you work towards resolving the problem.

Remember, becoming a proficient problem solver is a journey that requires time and practice. Embrace challenges, maintain persistence, and continuously seek opportunities to develop and refine your problem-solving skills. By adopting a proactive and solution-oriented mindset, you can effectively tackle problems and contribute to positive outcomes in various aspects of your life.

***

5) Power of sequence in marketing

Sequencing in marketing

The power of sequence in marketing refers to the strategic ordering and sequencing of marketing activities to create a more impactful and effective customer journey. By carefully planning the sequence of marketing messages and actions, businesses can guide customers through a series of steps that lead to desired outcomes, such as making a purchase, becoming a loyal customer, or advocating for the brand. Here are some ways in which the power of sequence can enhance marketing efforts:

1. **Awareness and attention:** The marketing sequence begins by capturing the attention of potential customers and generating awareness about your brand, product, or service. This can be achieved through targeted advertising, content marketing, social media campaigns, and various promotional strategies.

2. **Interest and engagement:** Once you have grabbed the attention of potential customers, the next step is to generate interest and engage them with your brand. This can involve providing valuable content, offering free resources or trials, hosting webinars or events, or encouraging interactions on social media platforms.

3. **Consideration and evaluation:** As customers become more engaged, they enter the consideration phase, where they actively evaluate your offerings. Here, the power of sequence comes into play by providing relevant information,

case studies, testimonials, and comparisons that help customers make well-informed decisions. Email marketing, personalized recommendations, and targeted nurturing campaigns can prove highly effective during this stage.

4. **Conversion and purchase:** The sequence reaches its climax as prospects are transformed into customers. By this stage, customers have gathered enough information and are ready to make a purchase. Offering incentives, implementing limited-time promotions, providing personalized offers, and a seamless purchasing experience can help drive conversions.

5. **Post-purchase experience:** The power of sequence extends beyond the purchase itself. It is important to continue engaging customers and providing a positive post-purchase experience. This can be achieved by sending order confirmations, providing relevant product usage tips, offering dedicated customer support, and actively seeking feedback to ensure customer satisfaction and encourage repeat purchases.

6. **Loyalty and advocacy:** Building customer loyalty and advocacy is another aspect where the power of sequence can be leveraged. By consistently delivering value, exceeding customer expectations, and nurturing relationships, businesses can turn satisfied customers into loyal brand advocates. This can involve loyalty programs, referral incentives, exclusive offers, and personalized communication to foster long-term customer loyalty.

7. **Upselling and cross-selling:** The power of sequence can also be applied to upselling and cross-selling efforts. Once a customer has made a purchase, strategic sequencing of relevant product recommendations, complementary offerings, and exclusive upgrades can effectively encourage customers to expand their purchase or explore new products.

8. **Customer lifecycle management:** Throughout the customer lifecycle, the power of sequence is instrumental in managing and nurturing relationships. By understanding the different stages of the customer journey, businesses can develop tailored marketing sequences and automation strategies that deliver the right messages at the right time, based on the customer's current stage.

The power of sequence in marketing enables businesses to guide customers through a purposeful and strategic journey, maximizing the effectiveness of marketing efforts and improving overall customer experience. By understanding the customer's needs, preferences, and behaviors at each stage, businesses can deliver targeted and relevant messages, build trust, and drive desired actions, ultimately leading to business growth and success.

***

6) Building great reputation

a) How to build authority in front of customer

Building authority in front of customers involves establishing credibility, expertise, and trust. Here are some strategies to help you build authority:

1. **Demonstrate knowledge and expertise:** Expand your knowledge and expertise within your industry or field. Stay updated on industry trends, research, and best practices. Share valuable insights, data, and case studies to showcase your expertise and position yourself as a trusted authority.

2. **Provide valuable content:** Create and share valuable content through various channels, such as blog posts, articles, videos, podcasts, or social media. Offer insights, tips, and practical solutions that address customer pain points and demonstrate your expertise. Consistently deliver high-quality, educational content that establishes you as a go-to resource in your industry.

3. **Speak at industry events:** Seek opportunities to speak at conferences, trade shows, webinars, or industry panels. By sharing your knowledge and insights in front of a relevant audience establishes your authority and enhances your visibility. Prepare engaging presentations and offer actionable advice to leave a lasting impression on attendees.

4. **Leverage customer testimonials and case studies:** Highlight success stories and positive customer experiences through testimonials and case studies. Testimonials from satisfied customers reinforce your authority by demonstrating your ability to deliver results. Case studies provide tangible evidence of your expertise and showcase how you've helped customers overcome challenges and achieve their goals.

5. **Engage in thought leadership:** Position yourself as a thought leader in your industry by sharing your unique perspectives, opinions, and insights. Publish articles in industry publications or contribute guest posts to reputable websites. Participate in industry forums, discussions, and social media groups to share your expertise and engage with peers and potential customers.

6. **Cultivate a professional online presence:** Build a professional online presence through a well-designed website, a strong LinkedIn profile, and active engagement on relevant social media platforms. Share valuable content, participate in discussions, and engage with your audience to establish yourself as an authority in your industry.

7. **Offer exceptional customer service:** Provide exceptional customer service that goes above and beyond customer expectations. Respond promptly to inquiries, address concerns effectively, and offer personalized assistance. Positive customer experiences contribute to your authority by generating word-of-mouth referrals and positive reviews.

8. **Be authentic and transparent:** Establish authority by being genuine, transparent, and ethical in your interactions with customers. Demonstrate integrity, honesty, and a genuine desire to help customers succeed. Authenticity builds trust and fosters long-term relationships with customers.

Remember, building authority is an ongoing process that requires consistency, dedication, and a genuine commitment to providing value to your customers. By establishing yourself as an authority, you position yourself as a trusted advisor and increase your influence in your industry.

***

7) Acknowledgement and Feedback

a) Power of Acknowledgment

The power of acknowledgment lies in its ability to validate, appreciate, and foster a deeper connection with others. When you acknowledge someone, you recognize their efforts, qualities, or achievements, which can profoundly impact their self-esteem, motivation, and overall well-being.

The power of acknowledgment in relation to customers cannot be overstated. Taking the time to acknowledge others and their contributions can have a profound effect on their lives and the overall dynamics of relationships and communities. Acknowledgment involves recognizing and appreciating the presence, needs, and concerns of customers. It plays a vital role in building strong relationships, enhancing customer satisfaction, and fostering loyalty. Here are some key aspects of its power:

1. **Validation and Respect:** Acknowledgment validates the significance of customers and their experiences. When customers feel heard and respected, it enhances their self-esteem and establishes a positive perception of the business. This, in turn, builds trust and fosters a deeper connection with the brand.

2. **Emotional Connection:** Acknowledgment recognizes the emotional aspect of customer interactions. It demonstrates empathy and understanding, conveying to customers that their feelings and concerns are valued. This emotional connection creates a positive customer experience and encourages ongoing business with the company.

3. **Customer Satisfaction:** Acknowledgment plays a crucial role in customer satisfaction. By promptly acknowledging their inquiries, feedback, or complaints, businesses demonstrate that their needs are being taken seriously. It establishes a foundation for effective problem-solving and ensures a smoother resolution process, resulting in higher level of satisfaction.

4. **Brand Loyalty:** When customers feel acknowledged, it cultivates a sense of loyalty towards the brand. They appreciate the effort made by the company to address their needs and concerns, which strengthens their bond with the business. Loyal customers are more inclined to make repeat purchases, recommend the brand to others, and remain loyal even in the face of competition.

5. **Word-of-Mouth and Reputation:** Acknowledgment has a significant impact on a company's reputation. Satisfied customers who feel acknowledged are more likely to share their positive experiences with others through word-of-mouth or online reviews. This, in turn, can attract new customers and enhance the overall reputation of the business.

6. **Competitive Advantage:** In a competitive market, acknowledgment can set a business apart from its competitors. Many companies overlook the power of acknowledgment, so by making it a priority, a business can differentiate itself and create a unique selling point. Customers are more likely to choose a company that values their input and provides personalized attention.

7. **Ripple effect:** Acknowledgment has a ripple effect, influencing not only the person being acknowledged but also those around them. When someone witnesses the positive impact of acknowledgement, they are more likely to adopt the practice and spread it to others, creating a cycle of positivity and support.

Overall, the power of acknowledgment lies in its ability to make customers feel valued, understood, and appreciated. It fosters a stronger relationship between businesses and their customers, leading to increased satisfaction, loyalty, and positive word-of-mouth.

b) How to take effective testimonial

Taking effective testimonials and ratings from your customers is essential for several reasons:

1. **Building trust and credibility:** Testimonials and ratings provide social proof and help establish trust with potential customers. Positive testimonials and high ratings demonstrate that others have had a positive experience with your product or service, increasing the confidence of new customers in choosing your business.

2. **Influence purchase decisions:** Testimonials and ratings can significantly influence the decision-making process of potential customers. Positive feedback from satisfied customers increases the likelihood of considering your offerings and making a purchase.

3. **Identifying strengths and weaknesses:** Testimonials and ratings provide valuable insights into what customers appreciate about your product or service. They highlight specific features, benefits, or experiences that resonate with customers, helping you identify your strengths. Additionally, negative feedback can shed light on areas that need improvement, allowing you to address any shortcomings.

4. **Marketing and promotional material:** Testimonials serve as powerful marketing tools. You can leverage them in various promotional materials, including your website, social media platforms, brochures, and advertisements. Genuine testimonials from satisfied customers help attract new customers and enhance your brand reputation.

To take effective testimonials and ratings, follow these guidelines:

1. **Timing:** Request testimonials when customers have had a positive experience with your product or service. This can be shortly after they've made a purchase, received excellent customer service, or achieved significant results through your offering.

2. **Make it easy:** Simplify the process for customers to leave testimonials and ratings. Provide a user-friendly and convenient method, such as a dedicated feedback form on your website, email surveys, or review platforms, to encourage customers to share their experiences.

3. **Ask specific questions:** Instead of vague or generic requests, ask customers specific questions that prompt detailed and meaningful responses. For example, inquire about how your product or service resolved a specific problem or surpassed their expectations.

4. **Use different formats:** Encourage customers to provide testimonials in various formats, such as written quotes, video testimonials, or audio recordings. This allows for diversity in testimonials and accommodates different preferences.

5. **Request permission and attribution:** Always ask customers for their consent to use their testimonials, and if possible, include their name, photo, or other identifying information. This adds authenticity and credibility to the testimonials.

6. **Follow up and express gratitude:** After customers provide testimonials or ratings, follow up with a personalized message to express gratitude for their feedback. Express your appreciation for their time and willingness to share their experience.

7. **Monitor and respond:** Regularly monitor customer testimonials and ratings across different platforms. Respond promptly to any negative feedback and address any concerns raised. Show that you value customer feedback and are committed to continuously improving your offerings.

Remember to comply with relevant regulations and guidelines regarding the use of testimonials and ratings in your industry or region. Always be transparent and genuine in your approach to gathering testimonials, as authenticity is key to building trust with your audience.

QUICK RECAP

In conclusion, this book is designed to empower you as a business champion in the field of Technology selling. Mr. Vohra and Mr. Arora transformed their mindset from zero to hero and generated more business which was more or less stagnant from many years. These 9 key pointers serve as invaluable guidance for every business owner striving to grow their business and establish a robust sales system. By following these guidelines, business owners can overcome challenges and set themselves on the path to growth and success. However, this is just the tip of the iceberg, as there is much more to learn and implement. Keep an eye out for the next version or book with the same title, where we delve deeper into the intricacies of the Technology world.

It's true that all the above pointers are interdependent and crucial for the success of a tech organization. They complement each other and help in building a strong foundation for growth. Without a defined market, it becomes challenging to operate, and streamlining the sales process becomes difficult. Clear terms, utilization of technology, and monitoring aid in ensuring the smooth functioning of the organization. Encouraging prompt response and offering multiple solutions help in collecting payments effectively. These elements work together to create a well-oiled machine that can drive growth and success for the business owner.

1. **New Age Mindset:** Embracing holistic growth and spirituality for personal transformation.

2. **Building Connections:** Cultivating meaningful relationships to foster success and fulfillment.

3. **Customer is the King:** Prioritizing customer needs and satisfaction for business prosperity.

4. **Be the Problem Solver:** Taking proactive steps to identify and resolve challenges for positive outcomes.

5. **Power of Sequence in Marketing:** Creating compelling marketing strategies and irresistible value propositions.

6. **Building Great Reputation:** Nurturing a solid reputation through integrity, excellence, and trust.

7. **Acknowledgment & Feedback:** Valuing feedback and acknowledging the contributions and perspectives of others.

TWO CHOICES

As an entrepreneur, you are constantly facing challenges and making decisions that can impact the future of your business. After reading this book, you now face a crucial choice. You can either continue operating as you have been, risking slow growth and missed opportunities, or you can choose to follow the 7 steps outlined in the book and take the steps towards a successful and thriving business.

As business owners, our father and we have experienced it all- the long hours, the stress, and the setbacks. I fully understand the difficulties and obstacles that come with running a business, and that's why we've written this book. Our goal is to shorten the journey of entrepreneurs like yourself, by sharing the valuable lessons we've learned from our 55+ years of combined experience.

Slow growth can pose a significant hurdle for any business and can lead to missed opportunities and a sense of frustration. However, it doesn't have to be that way. By following the 7 steps outlined in this book, you'll be able to identify and address the money-murdering mistakes that are holding you back, and take the necessary steps to grow your business.

Within these pages, you'll discover strategies for streamlining your sales and collection processes, leveraging the right technology, and implementing effective sales strategies. By addressing these key areas, you'll be equipped with the tools and insights necessary to achieve success while avoiding common pitfalls that often plague entrepreneurs.

The choice is yours. You can either continue on the path of slow growth, missed opportunities, and a lack of clarity in your business, or you can make a change today and embark on a journey towards success and growth. It's time to break free from the confines of a sales-less existence, limited connections, transaction-based communications, and a lack of security. It takes courage to make the difficult decisions, but the rewards of a thriving business are well worth it. So, take the first step, and allow us to guide you towards realizing your full potential.

Unlock Your Business's Potential with These 7 Steps and more.

"Starting with 15 mistakes, I have consolidated numerous key pointers to simplify the journey for distributors. However, there are still additional key factors that are crucial for reaching greater heights in the world of entrepreneurship. If you are eager to learn more and take your business to the next level, we (me and our team) cordially invite you to visit our office for a cup of tea or coffee. Our team would be happy to share our valuable insights and extensive experience with you.

A business that is not making progress is either declining or on the verge of stagnation. Alternatively, you can join me to propel your business to new heights in less than 3 months. Moreover, if you encounter any challenges or find yourself at a standstill during your business journey, we are here to support you. Our goal is to help you establishing a strong sales and collection system and achieving success in your distribution business. You can reach out to us at Atul@modiithub.com or anuj@modiithub.com, and we will do our best to assist you.

As a token of appreciation for your time and consideration, I would like to let you know that we are currently working on another book, a version 2.0 of the same title, "7 steps to Accelerate Your Business: Growth Hack. This new edition will expand upon the knowledge shared in this book, offering additional insights and strategies to help you succeed in the distribution industry. It may also include the more key factors.

Thank you once again for your time and consideration. I look forward to helping you achieve your goals.

NOTES:

NOTES: